52-Card Pickup

How COVID Made Magic Disappear

52-Card Pickup

How COVID MADE MAGIC DISAPPEAR

DAWN MORGAN

Cover photo by Kelsi Barnett at Kelsi Rae Photography
Back cover photo by Diana Lawrence
Author Photo by Andy Amyx Photography
Edited by David Bushman
Cover & Book design by Scott Ryan

Published in the USA by Fayetteville Mafia Press
Sarasota, Florida

Contact Information
Email: fayettevillemafiapress@gmail.com
Website: fayettevillemafiapress.com

ISBN: 9781949024357
eBook ISBN: 9781949024364

For: My mom, Carolyn Morgan, who raised me this way.

CONTENTS

FOREWORD

The pandemic has had immeasurable impact on so many different industries around the world, but perhaps none as dramatically as the live-entertainment industry. Literally overnight, bands and variety artists lost everything they had worked to build their entire lives. Every amusement park worldwide, every theater on Broadway and beyond, every casino in Las Vegas, and every nightclub on every street corner in every city were locked shut with no possibility of reopening for the foreseeable future. It is out of these chaotic and devastating times that *52-Card Pickup* was written. For people outside of the entertainment industry, it is hard to fully understand how shocking this situation truly was to those who have dedicated their lives to helping make other's lives happy through their performances.

Professional entertainers sacrifice everything to follow their passion. Relationships, children, family all suffer when you live the life of an entertainer. Being an entertainer is not a job, but rather a calling; entertainers do not choose but rather are compelled to follow their path. Most entertainers do not have the financial comfort zone that people working in "normal" jobs have—in fact, even some of the greatest performers of all time were broke and in debt when they passed away, including Michael Jackson and many others.

Entertainers do not have retirement programs, guaranteed work, or even healthcare. Most work from season to season and have just enough in the bank to carry them through the "dry season" each year. Much like farmers, entertainers plant the seeds (sell our shows) each year, wait for the crops to grow (bookings to arrive), and then take the crops to market: finally make the money, when they perform. Having said all of that, Dawn and her partner, Anthony, are arguably the most successful magicians and illusionists in the Southern California area, performing for decades at popular venues in the area, including Tom's Farms, Castle Amusement Park, and at the historic Welk Resort in Escondido, as well as upscale luxury hotels in Orange County and Palm Springs. Dawn and Anthony present more shows in a normal year than many other entertainers perform in ten years, so when the pandemic struck, it was literally an unimaginable psychological and financial shock on a deep emotional level for them. Had it been a nuclear bomb where everything was destroyed, the situation may on some level have been more understandable, but with the pandemic, entertainment venues were still standing there, silent, and the people who filled those venues were shuttered in a seemingly never-ending lockdown.

52-Card Pickup gives an in-depth, behind-the-scenes look at the trials and tribulations of professional entertainers during the COVID era, and how the pandemic inexorably altered the course of their dreams. It is a book of survival through a journey into uncharted dark waters. Ultimately it is a story of how the love of performing never dies and will once again succeed.

May 2021
MICHAEL MEZMER,
CERTIFIED CLINICAL HYPNOTHERAPIST

Michael Mezmer, Dawn Morgan, and Anthony
Hernadez at Welk Resort Theatre
Photo courtesy of Michael Mezmer

Dawn Morgan & Anthony Hernadez wait to go onstage in Palm Springs.
Photo by Jon Abeyta

INTRODUCTION

The year 2020 started off with a bang! Anthony and I had performed two magic shows on New Year's Eve 2019, and our 2020 calendar was filling up quickly. This was due in part to a new law in the state of California, AB5, or California Assembly Bill 5. Popularly known as the "gig worker bill," it took effect on January 1, 2020, and required companies that hire independent contractors to reclassify them as employees, with some exceptions. AB5 was designed to regulate companies that hire gig workers in large numbers, such as Uber, Lyft, and DoorDash.

This bill, however, also affected entertainers, landscapers, hairstylists, pool cleaners, and nail technicians. Anyone who hired a business or sole proprietor and did not put them on the payroll, thereby failing to deduct the necessary taxes, could be subject to penalty.

A top-performing magic act, we were AH Illusions, INC, incorporated in 2012 due to an audit by both the IRS and the state Employment Development Department. At the time, we felt like this would be the worst thing to happen to us.

For three years we were stressed. We had never been audited before. We did not know how this would end, how much money we would be fined, and what the end result would be. We had done nothing wrong with the exception of growing a business too fast. We provided taxes, documents, and receipts for all three years. We gathered advice. We prayed and bargained with the universe. We hired an amazing CPA, made the necessary changes, paid the fines to the EDD for hiring our magician assistants as "independent contractors," and finally we moved on.

In 2012 minimum wage in the state of California was eight dollars an hour. Adding in workmen's compensation insurance, unemployment insurance, the company's match on the individual retirement accounts, and all the other rules and stipulations, we did not know if we would be able to manage these additional costs, and continue to grow our business.

Anthony Hernandez, known as "Anthony the Magic," and I met at Castle Park in 2004. I had been hired to work at the local amusement park as its group sales manager. My job at Castle Park came to me purely by luck. I was working for Riverside Icetown, the local ice rink that sits behind Castle Park, and went to the amusement park to ask for a donation for the annual fundraiser I was hosting. I gave the marketing director my business card, and by the time I got home that evening, he had sent me an email asking me if I would be interested in a job. I politely turned him down, but he then asked me if I would just send in my résumé and come in to meet the general manager. This day would forever change the course of my life. I took the job as the group sales manager with the stipulation I could also keep the job at Riverside Icetown. Icetown was just around the corner, and I could easily jump back and forth between the two entities.

Castle Park was an easy sell, and my job was fun for me. I liked all of my coworkers, and we became a small family at work. Castle Park sits on twenty-five acres and features four eighteen-hole golf courses, thirty-two amusement park rides, and one very large arcade. I became the go-to girl for grad nights, company picnics, field trips, and football banquets.

Anthony was the park magician and had been there for nine years prior to my arrival. He was always there to help me out if I had a question about the park. Sometimes when booking groups for Castle Park, I would take Anthony with me to the meeting to "wow" the client with his magic and let them know his magic show was included in the cost of the ticket. Additionally, Anthony could perform a special show for their group at a separate cost. Anthony and I were friends from the start. OK . . . maybe he had a little crush on me...

I stayed at Castle Park from 2004 through 2007. In 2007 I had been booking Anthony outside of the park so much that push was coming to shove. And it was getting harder and harder for me to clock in my forty hours. We took the leap of faith and went out on our own as "Anthony the Magic Show." We still had our regular shows at Castle Park, but I was no longer its group sales manager.

Then, in 2012, the audit happened. For me, as a former actress, professional cheerleader, model, and sales girl, it was not a big deal to pay someone as an independent contractor. This is how magicians generally paid their assistants. I had always paid my own self-employment tax, so we did not understand why we were being audited. Things in California were changing, though, and this would be one of those changes.

I was offered salary and benefits to return to my former

position at Castle Park full-time. Since Anthony had been the magician at Castle Park for fifteen years now, we knew if I did a good job as an employee of the park, and watched my p's and q's, I could break away and help with the magic shows if he absolutely needed me. As the Castle Park group sales manager, I would sometimes work a grad night from 11:00 p.m. to 4:00 a.m., and therefore have a weekday of my choice off in exchange. My schedule was flexible in this way, to accommodate the groups I was bringing in. To survive this audit, I accepted the job offer. Our magic show schedule was rolling with a weekly rotation of regular venues. We had three great assistants at the time, so I took the position knowing I could manipulate my hours if Anthony had an "emergency."

As a former Girl Scout, I was always "prepared." This year would be no exception.

CHAPTER 1:

FOURTEEN DAYS

On March 12, 2020, Anthony and I woke up early and drove out to Anaheim, California, to perform for a "new to us" elementary school. There would be back-to-back performances for students who had exhibited good behavior. It was raining, and we left early in hope of getting to the school in time to load in during a break from the rain. So far, we had worked every day in March, and today's shows would mark numbers twenty-one and twenty-two in less than two weeks. We were to be "off" from magic on Friday, March 13, and our next day off on the books was to be April 1.

We had a great drive, which is rare for Southern California, and made it to the school early, with a break in the rain to load in. The school was lovely, the principal was excited, and the students were awesome to perform for. A few of them wore masks, but nothing else was out of the ordinary.

We had enough time to hang out backstage in the auditorium library and were intrigued by all the gifts from the Disney Company. We wished we could go to that school so that we could earn the Disney conductor's hat Anthony tried on for a photo op. We put the hat back on the shelf and got ready for the show. Lucky kids!!

Anthony has no idea Disney is about to announce the closure of its parks.
Photo by Dawn Morgan

After the two shows were finished, we loaded up and drove through lunch. I told Anthony to drop me off at Castle Park, where he had been performing magic shows for the past twenty-five years. I had not had time to clock in any work hours at the amusement park yet this week.

Anthony and I had met at Castle Park in 2004 when I became one of the park's group sales managers. We clicked from the start, and knew we wanted to work together outside of the park. "Anthony the Magic Show" was a natural fit for me. Once I made the introduction between Anthony and a potential client, the show was a breeze to sell. Before I knew it, we had a full schedule of appearances on the books. Once someone saw Anthony's show live, they would want him at their events too. One show led to another. It didn't take long before I was juggling multiple bookings for both Castle Park and "Anthony the Magic Show." Somewhere between working at Castle Park and planning the magic shows, Anthony and I became a couple. It was never really discussed or planned; we just started spending more and more time together. We sometimes joke that we share a brain.

In 2007, I left my position at Castle Park for the first time. We were booking more shows than we had assistants for. If I left my position at Castle Park, and focused only on the magic, I could possibly book even more shows. Then, while we were undergoing an audit for the years of 2009, 2010, and 2011, I saw an opportunity to return to the park in a part-time capacity. I read online that my replacement at Castle Park had left my former position. It was summer, and I was stressed about the financial ramifications of the impending audit. During the summer, our magic show schedule is more open, due to a lack of school shows. This would leave my days free to do what I wanted. I called the general manager,

Justin, with an offer to help out for the summer until they found a replacement for my replacement. My intention was not to stay at the park full-time, but to help out and make extra money during the summer. Castle Park offered me my old position back with a better salary and full benefits. After much discussion with Anthony, I took the offer. I would return to work at Castle Park for a second time in the group sales and marketing position. This time I would remain at the park from 2013 through 2017. I would once again leave Castle Park on good terms with management. It was known that the magic show would always take priority, and I wouldn't let Anthony down in this respect. I would be asked back again in 2019 to help in any way I could, even if we had to figure out a part-time rate. I returned to the park for a third time. As I said earlier, selling this park is easy for me. Why not?

On March 12, after our two school shows, Anthony dropped me off at the park so I could answer my phone calls and emails. Our birthday coordinator sat at the desk to my right, and our senior sales rep sat in front of me. It was a cozy office, just the three of us, and we all jelled. I noticed a frustration coming from our birthday coordinator, Yaritza, and this was not her normal demeanor. I continued to return calls, leave messages, and go through emails. I noticed my cell phone on my desk was blowing up, but I disregarded it and kept plugging away. As I said, I had not put in any hours yet that week, and needed to accomplish something that day. I really needed to answer all my phone calls and emails. I could never relax at Castle Park until I had booked something new and it was confirmed on paper. I knew I was the park's best sales and event person, and if I did not book something new every day, I felt like I had failed. If someone canceled an event for any reason, I felt the need to backpedal and book two events in its place.

Yaritza mentioned that almost all of her birthday parties for the weekend were canceling, but I thought it was due to the incoming rain. I had no idea that just moments before, Disney had made the decision, and the announcement, to close its parks. I turned over my phone to check, and I had several texts, voicemails, and emails that caused concern. Before listening to them, I went to the greatest source for news, Facebook.

Published March 12, 2020:

Every Disney theme park worldwide will be closed starting this weekend, including Disney World in Florida and the Disneyland Resort in California, because of the coronavirus pandemic, the company said on Thursday. Disney Cruise Line will also close.

Disneyland Park and Disney California Adventure — two adjoining, but separately ticketed theme parks in Anaheim, Calif. — will close on Saturday morning through the end of the month. Disney's three hotels in Anaheim will remain open until Monday.

My heart skipped a beat, and suddenly I realized this was real. I went back to my Castle Park email inbox and could not keep up with the number of emails that were coming in. At my desk, the group sales line for Castle Park started to blow up. My cell phone was vibrating on my desk. I did not answer any of it. April, Yaritza, and I sat there in disbelief and knew it would not be long before our general manager, Ken, and our assistant general manager, Heather, would make it up to our office.

Anthony had been texting me asking if I was OK and if I had heard the news. I was OK and I had heard the news, but my mind was scrambling and processing. I told him to come pick me up in an hour. Ken and Heather came up to our office to ask if we had heard the announcement. We told them we had, and the phones were ringing off the hook. We all agreed this weekend was going to be a wash, with the pending rain. We would take this time to process what was going on before answering any more calls or emails. Let's call it a day and regroup tomorrow.

To add to the stress of what happened on Thursday, March 12, April's last day at Castle Park after twenty-some years was to be the following day, Friday the thirteenth. I was assured that with her leaving the park to move to Tennessee, I would be needed more than ever, since I was the only one who knew that department. Her replacement had not been locked in yet, and I felt confident that for me financially, life would be OK.

Meanwhile, just like in a poorly scripted movie: cue the ominous rain on Friday the thirteenth and let the festivities begin. We had gone from performing over six hundred shows a year for sixteen straight years to being completely out of work in just one afternoon.

Thu, Mar 12, 2020, 1:44 PM

Good afternoon Anthony,

Our school district has notified all Central Schools in our area that all events must be postponed until further notice due to pandemic health concerns with the COVID-19.

I will contact you immediately to set a new date for our Magic Show here at XXXX Elementary once the ban is lifted.

Thank you,
XXXX
Co-President

Thu, Mar 12, 2020, 2:39 PM

Hi Anthony,

I have just received word that we are going to postpone or possibly cancel our Easter event due to everything going on with the Coronavirus. In case of postponement, and if you are available, would you be willing to come out and still perform for us? As soon as I get word on a possible date, I will get back to you. I am sorry for any inconvenience this may cause. 😞 If you have any questions or concerns, please feel free to contact me.

Thank you!
XXXX
Recreation Supervisor

Good Evening Anthony & Dawn,

I regretfully am reaching out to inform you that our General Manager, under policies placed by XXXX Worldwide, has made the decision to cut all large gathering events at our resort in response to the coronavirus outbreak. We will have to cancel all upcoming shows for the months of March & April. I sincerely apologize as this is a difficult time for us all. Thank you for understanding.

Sincerely,
XXXX

CHAPTER 2:

THE ICING ON THE CAKE

Anthony and I went home from Castle Park on Thursday, March 12, 2020 and were very solemn. We were all we had, and although I am the doomsayer in the relationship, today I had to be Pollyanna. I assured Anthony we had worked all those years, and all of those shows, and reminded him of our agreement on the first day we met and decided to work together. On that day I had told him that in entertainment you always take shows and never turn them away, because one day there will not be shows. It is then you will rest and not feel guilty or bad that you did not work when you had the chance. We took that to heart in our business and knew we had to strike while we were hot. For sixteen years, we accommodated every show we could before our luck ran out, before we got to be too old, or too ugly.

When I first met Anthony at Castle Park in 2004, he had been there for nine years as both the park magician and an employee of the park. I did not know when I met him that he was a forty-hour-a-week hourly employee with partial benefits. He had worked his way up from being the host in the big top to convincing the owner of the park, Bud Hurlbut, to let him do a few magic tricks for the birthday parties that came in. Bud Hurlbut was famous in the amusement park arena, as he had created the Calico Mine and Timber Mountain Log Rides for Knott's Berry Farm. He was good friends with both Walter Knott and Walt Disney. Castle Park looks like a "mini me" of Knott's Berry Farm, with a few nods to Disneyland, including the apartment that oversaw the park, where Bud had lived before passing away in 2011.

Anthony and I made a great dinner that evening that included food we normally do not eat, as we are always trying to stay fit and healthy for the show. The only thing I remember about the dinner is the two kinds of ice cream in the extra-large bowl that we drowned our sorrows in. I assured Anthony we had savings, and that is why we had worked so hard, and we always make our house payments a month in advance, so we were OK. Fourteen days to a month would not be a problem. We would take this time to do all the things we needed to get accomplished, so moving forward we were ready for the world!

The next morning, we got busy! I had Anthony take all the dry cleaning in, so that when these two weeks were up, our clothes would be perfect and ready to go. Next, we dropped off our best truck at the mechanic on the way to April's goodbye party. We left it for an oil change and a look-see to ensure we would be road ready in two weeks! We went to Castle Park, which could have remained open for this final weekend, however . . . it was raining. When it rained, two of our regular venues, Tom's Farms and Castle Park, would generally close. This would mean we would have the weekend off.

Once inside Bud's former apartment at Castle Park, which was now the general manager's office, we realized life had changed overnight. The people I had sat in an office with the day prior, I was now to stay six feet back from, and did I have a mask? It was a nice party, and since I had two weeks off from my "diet," I had two halves of Jersey Mike's subs and two Bundt cakes, one chocolate and one vanilla.

Anthony and I went home and talked about all the things we were going to tick off our list over the next two weeks. We started organizing the magic in my garage. We also called our landscapers and canceled their service for the next month. I canceled the mobile dog groomer. I cannot justify paying someone to do something for me that I can do for myself if I am not working . . . and based on the stack of emails I had . . . I was not going to be working!

Saturday and Sunday we spent our time at the gym, we went to boot camp, and we climbed Mount Rubidoux. If I was going to be eating ice cream and cupcakes, I should really work it off. I vowed that in the next two weeks I would get into the best shape of my life! We also started watching the full series of *Mad Men*, and it was really addicting. We had worked so much over the past sixteen years, we never had the chance to finish a program, see a season finale, or find out what happened on any show we had started watching.

Monday I went to Castle Park to print out all the emails and write down all the voicemail messages in my box. Anthony went with me to clean his stage, mop the floors, organize backstage, and assess what we had there for shows. He took down the curtains so we could have them cleaned. We were on fire. Four days down, maybe ten left to go . . . right?

On the way to Castle Park, Anthony had told me he

Our annual show in Snowflake, Arizona—canceled.
Photo by Diana Lawrence

applied for unemployment insurance on Sunday night when he could not sleep. I was so upset for two reasons: 1) He did it without me, and what about me? 2) Since we are incorporated, don't we pay for that? I had never been unemployed in my life, and I honestly did not know how it worked. The CPA we had hired during the audit had said we needed to pay the UI (unemployment insurance) tax, and we paid it. My thoughts at the time were just to keep me from being audited or going to jail. What is the bill? For the past five to fifteen years, life had been coming at me so hard and so fast I could barely keep my head above water, so I just took all the advice I could and trusted those I hired to take care of things I could not.

I did know from my mom being on unemployment when she would get laid off from her "good factory job" that you had to do a job search to qualify. We had been watching the newscasts, and they mentioned "essential workers" were needed. I told Anthony that I had worked for the local grocery store chain, Stater Bros., right after high school, and I still had my union card. I may be able to get a job there. We logged onto our computers, and we both applied. Next, Anthony thought of Amazon. We applied there and were hired on the spot!! In five days, we went from unemployed to Amazon associates. I will forever be grateful to this company for this opportunity. On Thursday, March 19, we went to the Amazon interview to get our photos taken and for a drug test (did not happen due to COVID) and orientation. We were to be part time, working four-hour shifts. We chose the 11:15 p.m. to 3:15 a.m. shift. Our logic was that when we went back to work, we could still work at Amazon, after our magic shows, and if we got to bed by 4:00 a.m., we could still work shows during the day on limited sleep. They asked if we wanted four, five, or six shifts a week. We took six, in case there was not another opportunity for work. Basically, we took every day except for Saturday, because, hey . . . Saturdays were for the magic shows.

We felt guilty about taking these jobs for only two to four weeks, but we agreed we would try to keep them if we could because Amazon had given us a job and an opportunity during this horrible time.

We felt pretty good about ourselves. We had picked up extra income, I still had a part-time job at Castle Park, we were working out, and we were accomplishing. Dry cleaning

. . . check. Cars repaired . . . check. Animals vaccinated . . . check. I had even made the choice to pay off the truck. I did not want any debt in front of me, and our savings were decent, so I wrote the check for three thousand dollars and some change and paid off the truck. It had been five years since my mother passed, and in that time there had not been one phone call on her landline that was not a bot. I canceled the landline. Check.

CHAPTER 3:

APRIL FOOLS

April 1 hit, and we were receiving money from unemployment and also being paid by Amazon. We felt good that we had jobs that would take some of the burden off our unemployment insurance, and that we could be saving this for another time, but hopefully not another emergency.

Our financial adviser, Paul Smith, had called to check in on us. He had been my mother's adviser and was like a dad to us. We told him we were OK and that we had taken jobs at Amazon. He told us how proud he was of us and asked if we wanted to rearrange any of our money in our IRAs. We told him no, and what goes down must also go up, and we would stay where we were. I was so happy to hear from Paul, and him telling me he was proud of me was like hearing it from my mother. He had been good to her when she was diagnosed with stage-four cancer. He visited her, prayed for her, spoke at her service when she passed, and then immediately called me to let me know what the next step was regarding the money in her accounts.

Life was good. The endless to-do list of errands was

complete, and the *Mad Men* binge on Netflix was a great mental break. It took me back to the 1960s, which, for some reason, I have strong memories of, despite my being born at the tail end of 1965.

I was, however, furloughed from Castle Park. My hourly rate there is pretty good, significantly more than I make at Amazon, but hey, I can pick up extra shifts at Amazon, and Anthony and I had been selling magic tricks online with some success. We were also selling items we no longer needed and cleaning out our houses.

Getting our driver's licenses renewed during COVID . . . check!!
Photo by Dawn Morgan

April 10 came, and I needed to pay my property taxes. My mom always took great pride in her bill-paying reputation and paying her bills on time. I had the money in the bank. This was not the problem. The problem was all the buildings were closed due to COVID. I went on the website and tried to pay with my credit card, but they wanted to charge a three hundred dollar fee for using the credit card! If I did not pay that day, I was going to be late, and then there would be a late fee! Tears, panic, and now one of the worst days of my life.

Before my mother passed five years ago, I overheard her telling a friend she had left enough money in the bank to get me through a year. After that, she did not know what I would do. Five years later I still had that money in her bank account. I will be damned if COVID is going to change that!! Anthony, who knew the gravity of the situation, came over to my house midtantrum. He had an ATM card (something I do not subscribe to), and he went down and paid the bill at the kiosk with only a $1.50 charge for the debit card. I transferred the money into his bank account. Crisis averted, for the moment.

CHAPTER 4:
SHOULD I STAY OR SHOULD I GO?

A
♥

♣
∀

A
♠

∀

By now it was April 13. One entire month had passed, and we were still working hard at Amazon. We had learned you could pick up as many shifts as you wanted with something called VET (Voluntary Extra Time). We could work up to sixty hours a week. We started to work more than six nights a week and agreed we needed better shoes to walk around on the concrete floors of Amazon. Some nights we would clock in sixty thousand steps. Our legs and backs were killing us from pulling the pallets from the conveyor belt to the truck-staging area. We each bought a pair of Asics and felt like we were walking on clouds. Now we could work more. We also realized that each shift was not just four hours, but could "flex up" to five or even six hours, so with six shifts a week, we were regularly working thirty to thirty-six hours, but still making significantly less than we did performing magic shows. Nonetheless, we would always talk about how lucky we were to have this job, and how lucky we were that soon we would be back performing magic shows again. We felt badly for our coworkers and newfound friends for whom

No one would believe how many steps we logged each night.
Photo by Anthony Hernandez

this was, at the time, their only option for employment.

Another thing that started to happen in April was all the entertainers on Facebook were jumping onto something called Zoom, to perform virtual shows. We agreed that we did not think we could do the same quality show on Zoom that we did live, and we would continue to wait it out and refer our virtual-show requests to friends who were performing on Zoom. After all, we had jobs at Amazon.

I had also toyed with the idea of moving to Tennessee. I had wanted to move to Maryville, Tennessee, since my mother left. She was the only thing holding me in California, and now the only reason to stay was the great income we made performing in the magic and illusion shows. We had life in California completely nailed down. We knew how to get the best concert tickets, the days to hit the best fairs, when to go skiing, when to go to the beach, and how to get consistent work.

Two houses on my block had sold during COVID, and they were very dated. Almost every homeowner on my street had lived here since the houses went up in the 1970s. Miss Jan and Miss Kay lived side by side, and after Miss Jan's house sold so quickly, Miss Kay's family used the same realtor to sell her house. It sold just as quickly. I had the realtor come over to hear what he had to say, and I thought his offer on my house was a little low. I had a ton of updates. I told him I would consider it and let him know. In the meantime, I had been preparing my house just in case. I spent all my spare time in lockdown pulling weeds, planting flowers, repainting the halls and baseboards, and cleaning. Before I could even think about the possibility of signing with the realtor, the house across the street from me, which is updated like mine, and has the same floor plan, went on the market. They listed the house for the same price I had in my head for my own house. I decided to sit back and watch.

We had been talking with one of our best friends, hypnotist Michael Mezmer. He told us he had been working at something called Instacart. He was a little older than we were, and Amazon for him was not an option, as the work was very laborious. Instacart sounded like something we could do, so Anthony signed up first, and we decided to do it together on his account. That Saturday we got up, got dressed, put the ice chests in our car, and set off to the grocery store. It was fun!! Kind of like an Easter egg hunt when the product pops up on your phone and you must go find it in the store. We did a couple of shopping trips together and decided we liked it. We also decided to get an Instacart on my phone and to divide and conquer. More money, more money, more money!!

Our days were now spent waking up, working out, doing a few Instacart trips, eating lunch, taking a nap, and then going to Amazon. We had a pretty good routine down. We felt very blessed to have jobs, our bills paid, and good friends like Michael Mezmer.

Finally, we came to the end of April. For years both Anthony and I had rented rooms in our houses to grad students at University of California, Riverside. This served as additional income, and we were also planning on our future. These two houses would be our nest egg when we were older and unable to perform magic shows. My mother had passed away in 2015 leaving her home to me. I didn't want to sell it at the time, so I rented out the spare bedrooms to grad students at UC Riverside. I kept the master bedroom so I could keep control of the house. The grad students were easy because their lives were all about sleeping and studying. Additionally, when Anthony and I would travel on cruise ships, or go on tour, we had someone at the house, so no one would break in. Anthony was also renting rooms at his house to help pay down the mortgage. My roommate, Soledad, had already given me her thirty-day notice at the beginning of the month. On April 15, Anthony received notice from his roommate. We understood. It makes no sense to rent a room in a house for the purpose of attending a college when that college does not have in-person classes, but instead online classes. Just another hit in the COVID CRISIS. Now, to add to our situation, we had not only lost our professional income, but our rental income as well. We refunded their deposits and wrote them letters of recommendation for when this crisis would be over. I would hope to get my roommate back, as she was AWESOME. However, I know that after this semester she would be going on to medical school, and not at UC Riverside.

CHAPTER 5:

MAYDAY!

I am not going to lie; the month of May was hard. We had a fantastic illusion show planned for a senior community in Roseville, California. We had performed to a standing ovation there in the year prior, and now they had to cancel this year. It had now been two months of lockdown, not fourteen days, as originally planned.

In 2020 we were also booked to perform in Colorado for the first time ever. We were going to perform in two different communities, on back-to-back nights, and both of those shows were canceled. Not only did we lose those shows, but we had to refund the deposits. Our bank account was losing as much steam as we were.

Our regular weekly shows that were going to resume in April, and then in May, were now sending us emails of cancellation until further notice.

Hey Dawn & Anthony,

I'm just writing to let you know the Activities department has been put on furlough until further notice. If you need to reach out to me, please call my cell phone (XXX-XXX-XXXX) as XXX and I will be losing our access to our work emails for the time being. You can also contact our boss XXXX at XX@XXX.com if you have any questions!

Hope you are doing well and staying safe and healthy!

XXXX

Thu, May 21, 2020, 6:50 PM

Anthony,

We are holding 6/27 as a new start date. However,... monitoring.

XXXX

Sent from my iPhone

We attended the birthday party of a little girl whom we had friended at one of our venues, Tom's Farms. Adeline and her mother, Terri, made regular appearances at our shows, and Terri had asked if we could stop by Adeline's birthday party that Saturday. We did not know what to expect at a lockdown birthday, but we bought a small gift, grabbed our masks, and went over. It was a nice, small gathering, with pizza and cake. Adeline seemed to like her gift, a face-painting kit, since she always had visited the face painter,

Call me J.Lo.
Photo by Dawn Morgan

Candy Clown, at Tom's Farms.

We also had called up one of our friends, PS Lola, an out-of-work drag queen and hairstylist from Palm Springs. Lola was "Queen of the Desert," and very glamorous. Lola worked as a hairstylist at all the major events in the desert and regaled us with stories of great beauties, including Jennifer Lopez. We needed to have our hair styled and cut, and Lola came right over to my house and did our hair on my back patio. A great cut for Anthony, and blonde highlights and a great cut for me. We felt like a million bucks! Call me J.Lo.

On May 20 we got a call for a private show on July 4. WHAT?!! Yes!! Of Course!! It had been more than two months and we had been good sports about the whole thing, but let us go!! I took that piece of optimism and decided to touch base with all our resorts that had dates on the books for 2020 before committing to the July 4 show. I did get responses back from two resorts that wanted to book us for the holiday. We would be outside with social distancing and masks. Yes!! We can do that. Sold!

We were glad this was now going to be over, and life would go back to normal.

Did I speak too soon?

CHAPTER 6:
1967

On May 25, a terrible event happened, as we witnessed on the news. It coincided with other terrible events, setting a nation that was already anxious and unsettled on fire.

George Floyd, a forty-six-year-old Black man, was killed in Minneapolis on May 25, 2020, while being arrested for allegedly using a counterfeit bill. During the arrest, Derek Chauvin, a White officer with the Minneapolis Police Department, knelt on Floyd's neck for about nine and a half minutes after he was handcuffed and lying face down. Two police officers, J. Alexander Kueng and Thomas Lane, assisted Chauvin in restraining Floyd, while another officer, Tou Thao, prevented bystanders from interfering with the arrest and intervening as events unfolded

People were angry, and the mood was palpable.

We are in no way equating this with the roots of the social turbulence that was consuming the country, but at the same time we were dealing with a very personal crisis. Anthony said he thought Sweet Pea, our fifteen-year-old show dog, may need to be put down. We were on our way to the veterinarian, and we were both very upset and frustrated. We got into a heated argument that resulted in canceling the vet appointment, and we decided to take Sweet Pea to Tom's Farms for "one last day" before making any big decisions. We stopped to buy "Wee" a cheeseburger and trespassed onto the Tom's Farms picnic grounds. Wee had grown up at Tom's Farms, where we had performed magic shows on Saturdays and Sundays for the past sixteen years. Despite being blind and deaf, Wee knew his way around every tree in the picnic area. We loved on him, took photos with him, and fed him his cheeseburger. He seemed to pep up and no longer needed the vet. I guess Wee just needed a break from all the isolation as well. We all needed this day. I wish everyone in the United States would have taken this one day.

Anthony and Sweet Pea at Tom's Farms
Photo by Dawn Morgan

What happened next was unthinkable. People started to protest. Nonviolent protest, just like in the days of Dr. Martin Luther King, Jr., but as night fell and frustrations grew, the protests turned into riots. Late on evening of Sunday, May 31, we were on our way to work at Amazon in San Bernardino. When we put the location in Waze, it told us to take a different route from the one we normally do. We felt that was odd, but as we got closer, we realized San Bernardino was in the midst of major upheaval. The streets were on fire, and we were told by the California Highway Patrol to turn around and go home. We were told to call our human resources director to say we were not going to make it to work that night. Our HR was very understanding and excused us for the night. We told our HR about our friends we were texting with who would not be able to make it there either because they were stuck in the mobbed streets and could not move their cars out.

The anger in people was very upsetting to me, and everyone's mood was heated.

I silently prayed and asked for direction. The next evening, I called off from Amazon again, as we had been told the riots were coming to Riverside on Monday, June 1. I will say the Riverside Police Department and our amazing sheriff, Chad Bianco, did a great job. They closed all the freeway ramps to the city and were prepared for something similar to what had happened in San Bernardino the night before. Our city got by with very little damage in comparison.

I stayed home that night and decided to go through some of my mother's things to see what I could "purge" in case I was going to move. April from Castle Park had told me the thing to do before moving was to get rid of what I did not want to pack, and to start packing up what I wanted to keep.

As if my mother knew I needed guidance that night, I found a *Time* magazine from 1967(see below). It was all about the race riots in Detroit. It was calming, but then I was angered as well. Why are we still having these same issues in America fifty years later?

From the collection of Dawn Morgan

CHAPTER 7:

THIS HAS TO BE A JOKE!

In June, Anthony and I became "blue badges" at Amazon. This is where we have passed the ninety-day probation mark and are bona fide Amazon employees. We were no longer seasonal. We now get full vision and dental, but . . . no one told us, and we will not figure that one out for a few months.

We were also made "learning ambassadors." Thanks to all our hard work carrying double pallets all night long and lifting the non-cons (boxes too heavy to put on the conveyor belt), and to always showing up, we now get to train all the new hires coming into LGB5, a sorting center, or the stop between the fulfillment center, where the orders are boxed, and the post office. This is where we receive inbound packages, place them on conveyor belts, scan them to the appropriate postal pallet, wrap and label the pallets, and finally stage the pallets to the outbound trucking lanes.

Anthony and I were awarded our bright neon-yellow and teal-blue vests that said "Ambassador" on the back. As we walked around the warehouse that night, we were lauded with congratulations from everyone we passed. We felt like rock stars.

Additionally, Castle Park sent me an email on June 26 asking if I could come back part-time, ten hours a week, on Tuesdays and Thursdays. Yes, sir!

Newly Minted Learning Ambassadors
Photo by Dawn Morgan

Sweet Pea has been seen by a vet and is feeling better. The sun is shining. Life is good.

I had tasked Anthony with calling his attorney to revise his will and trust. His mother had passed in 2018, and I was the only name left on his will. What if we got into a car accident together? Who would speak for us if we could not? God forbid, if we were to pass, who would take care of our animals? Provisions must be made.

Anthony called me to let me know our attorney told him

our financial adviser, Paul Smith, had been arrested and charged with arranging a ten-million-dollar Ponzi scheme. Anthony relays this information to me, and I absolutely do not believe him. Not Paul. Paul who is like a father to me. Paul who was at my mom's bedside when she passed. Paul who spoke at her service. Paul who called to say how proud he was that we got jobs at Amazon. I blew it off as gossip. There was just no way. However, this ended up being the truth. Just when life cannot get any more unreal, I called Paul, but his voicemail was full. I then called my mother's friend Margie. It was true. He had taken $50,000 from her. I immediately went into the obsessive/compulsive process of checking all my accounts, my employees' accounts, Anthony's accounts, and, most importantly . . . my mother's accounts. I think for some reason Paul really liked my mother, and therefore her account was safe. Or she was looking out for me, as she generally does. I cannot wait to have a conversation with her about all of this. Oh Mom . . . why did you leave me?

June continued to sail along. We did a few live shows, and after we had turned down many requests for Zoom virtual shows, we got one we could not turn away. We booked a Zoom virtual show for five different military bases that were joining together to entertain the families who could not leave the base. We decided we were going to put our best foot forward, and had been taking notes on what did and did not work when we watched other performers' Zoom shows. We tried every camera we had, every backdrop, every sound system, every microphone, and finally . . . we felt like we were ready to go. I am not going to lie: we went through a booking agent, and we probably did not charge him enough. We had called a few friends, as this was unknown territory, and we asked what they were charging. We were told half of

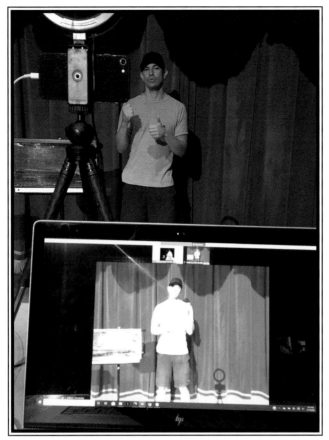

Our virtual reality
Photo by Dawn Morgan

what the show would normally be live. The agent probably made two house payments off that show, but for us, we put our foot in the water and we survived. We were excited now at this new possibility. For us, that was paid practice with a great audience.

I had been toying with the idea of making the Zoom show better, and the only idea I could come up with was to mix in more than one entertainer to keep the energy levels high.

As if it came from my mouth to God's ears, Kevin Johnson

dials my phone. Kevin and Anthony had performed "Comedy & Magic" at Welk Resort Theatre, and honestly, I had not seen a show with their energy in many years and have not seen a show that fun since Kevin left Welk to perform on cruise ships.

Kevin had mentioned his wife, Cherie, said he should call me and see if I could book him into shows. I told him I was not even booking Anthony at this point, but I had this great idea. Kevin said if I could make it happen, he would pay me 10 percent or whatever. He just had five kids to feed and needed to work. I told him to send over his press kit and let me see what I could figure out. This for me would be a whole new business, a whole new start, and I do not do well at failing, so . . . give me some time.

Since we had furloughed our magician assistants, I had the idea when we went back to the Welk Resort Theatre in June that we would split our pay with Kevin, and he could help us with the illusions. Plus, since he would take up half of the showtime, we would take only half of the illusions. Therefore, I did not need to worry about having assistants. We would of course choose the illusions we could perform alone, without additional assistants. Welk had been pushed back from the June 27 date and was now looking at a July start date. Additionally, who knows what illusions would still be in working order after sitting in storage for months, and which ones may need to go to prop repair?

CHAPTER 8:

INDEPENDENCE DAY

July Fourth weekend came and went so quickly, but we were working!! I had discovered that the Christian schools had not closed, and they in fact did need a school assembly to reward students for good behavior.

I had also called all the venues we had been performing at weekly prior to COVID and suggested doing a virtual show for both on-property and off-property guests, "Anthony the Magic LIVE."

Castle Park, always our champion, gave us this opportunity. On July 18 we performed our first "Anthony the Magic LIVE from Castle Park" virtual show. The park used this show as a tool to promote that it was once again open for miniature golf, outside, socially distanced, with masks and temperature checks. Castle Park paid us, and the show was free to anyone on its Facebook page, season ticket holders, and guests.

We booked a few high-end shows for people who were sick of being locked up. These people had enough money and enough property to really put on the dog. Anthony and I gladly took our show anywhere they wanted to throw their events. We were starting to feel normal again.

All the entertainers I had seen on Facebook were promoting their Zoom virtual shows to potential audiences on Facebook and Eventbrite, and selling tickets to view their shows. They would set a date and sell the tickets for twenty dollars a household. That seemed like a good idea, but they could market only to people they knew or who came across their feed on social media.

I had a better idea. If Anthony and Kevin were to host a FREE showcase for all entertainment bookers, we would be doing one FREE show for those who make the booking decisions. We set the date for Monday, August 3, at 7:00 p.m. I started to contact everyone in my Rolodex who may have a need for a virtual show. It is very hard to promote a show without any promotional materials, but we did it. We decided

Trying to entertain the audience at a distance
Photo by Dawn Morgan

to host a practice show for our friends and family to get our timing and sound down. The problem with the practice show was the audience was looking at us with a critical eye. They were all friends and family and had all seen our shows before. They all wanted to give us feedback and were taking notes and not enjoying it like a regular audience. Without applause and laughter, we were a little disheartened, but we took their great feedback, implemented it, and decided we would need to do a shot of alcohol before the showcase on August 3.

Meanwhile, California was to shut down again, and I was once again furloughed from Castle Park, on July 31. To add to that, the Welk Resort Theatre show was now being pushed to August.

Creative audience participation
Photo by Dawn Morgan

CHAPTER 9:
SHOWCASE

Monday, August 3, came, and we were ready for a showcase. Kevin had called in Paul Beach, our sound director from Legoland, and Kevin's sound was stellar. Anthony and I wished we had had time to work with Paul before the showcase, but we were confident we were going to do a good show. Kevin had been having trouble deciding on a background. Should he go with a virtual background, a green screen, a regular backdrop? So we were happy he felt confident with his sound. We performed the showcase and felt the love from those who watched. This time, there was laughter and applause. (Thank God and Thank you, Absolut Vodka).

Anthony and I got on the horn with Paul Beach the very next day to see what we could do to improve our sound. We had another Castle Park virtual show coming up that weekend, and we wanted to up our game too.

In August we are normally signing our contracts for the coming year, booking school shows and resorts. Our Christian schools had called and asked if we could do a different show or if we knew of any other entertainers who could perform. I of course booked Kevin, and then referred animal magician John Abrams. I did not take a fee, as I have always been taught to pitch in and help others. Kevin helped us with our sound by bringing in Paul, and John helped me get over the Zoom hump in the beginning by letting us sit in on one of his shows. John had been one of the top school-show magicians pre-COVID but was now teaching online classes for a magic school he created.

Some of the booking agents who did not attend our showcase told us we had held it too late in the day. This was especially true for those on the East Coast. We quickly set another showcase date for Tuesday, August 18, at 1:00 p.m., and went to work on promoting that.

While we were very motivated to promote and work out our virtual show, we were losing steam at Amazon LGB5. At the end of June, we had put in a schedule request to drop down from six nights a week to five. This request went

The Ultimate Virtual Variety Show
Photo created by Kevin Johnson

denied for the remainder of our time at LGB5. We loved it there, and we loved the people, but we were so tired and discombobulated from working the night shift. Our sleep was off. We would get home around 5:00 a.m. Then, with the sun coming up, we would be too wound up to sleep right away. We would sleep a few hours, run our errands, eat lunch, take a nap, wake up for dinner, maybe take another hour-long nap, and go back to work. Our sleep consisted of two to three naps a day when we could get them in. Sometimes we would wake up and not know what we woke up for, why, what day it was, or if we had overslept, which would send us into a panic.

There was a new Amazon ONT1, also a sorting center, opening in September, and the company was asking if anyone wanted to transfer. Anthony and I signed up, as we saw it as the only way to get out of the six-night-a-week grind. We were tired, our bodies were tired and breaking down, and we were COVID tired.

CHAPTER 10:

DON'T TOUCH MY HAIR

In September we set our sights on taking a six-month break. We had been working hard and felt we deserved some time off, and we needed the mental break. Anthony's birthday is in July, and originally we had bought tickets to go see the Go-Go's concert at Humphreys Concerts by the Bay in San Diego. The concert was canceled, and we put in for a refund from Ticketmaster. We had been advised by email to apply for the refund quickly. We did, and we were denied. The concert had been "rescheduled" for 2021, and therefore tickets were not being refunded. We were told we should have bought the insurance. All I know is a pandemic is an "Act of God," and in an "Act of God" contracts are no longer valid. Refund my money! I am unemployed and you are Ticketmaster. After much argument, we finally did get a refund. Many people who purchased tickets to various concerts had to fight to get a refund. I think Ticketmaster is horrible for doing that to people who are out of work. I know some people went to the fan sites for the performers they had purchased tickets to see and let those performers know the situation. One performer refunded their money. Chris Stapleton sent emails to his fans, and his fans received a refund through his fan website. Chris Stapleton is a stand-up guy. Ticketmaster can suck it.

I saw online the Utah State Fair was still going to happen in September 2020, with REO Speedwagon and Styx as the headliner acts. I was so excited I called the fair directly to ask about cancellations and refunds, and I bought the tickets with confidence for September 14. This would be our perfect six-month, small trip. Utah was drivable, and we had driven through the state in 2019 to go to Glenwood Springs, Colorado. We knew the drive would be beautiful.

We had heard Utah and Idaho were open, and we were excited to get out of town. I will say Utah was more open than California, but the hotel was disappointing. There was no breakfast due to COVID, and I did not think to even ask if that would be taken off the table when I booked my room. In my opinion, the hotel should have had breakfast from 7:00 to 9:00 a.m. and given you a checklist so that you could pick three items to be delivered to your room at a specific time. Something like coffee, hard-boiled eggs, Danish, cereal and milk, fruit, yogurt, or juice.

Then, the topper: the spa was closed due to COVID.

We stayed to check out the fair, but we arrived way too early. It was baking hot, and there was literally no one there. We like to visit the vendors at fairs, so to get out of the heat we put this first, before food, rides, and hopefully some form of entertainment. As we walked through the air-conditioned halls, the vendors were aggressive for sales. More so than usual. One lady grabbed my hair to start curling it (which I hate, curly hair on me), and then her partner put oil in her hands and came up to put the oil in my hair, with me protesting all the while. I had literally just washed and straightened my hair and did not plan to wash it again the next day, as we were going to go rafting in Lava Hot Springs. I told the vendor to relax and let me look around, as I had just arrived at the fair and wanted to see everything. We got into a spat about how she has not worked since March. I replied, "Neither have I."

Rafting fun in Lava Hot Springs, Idaho
Photo by Dawn Morgan

I get it with the vendors: the hope of going to another state, one that is "open," and paying for a booth at a fair to make an income from your sales. The desperation was too much for me, and we left so that I could go back to the hotel and watch *Dancing with the Stars*. I spent the night depressed for both the vendors at the fair and myself.

Idaho was way more open, and we had a blast!! If hindsight were 2020 (just a joke), I wish we would have gone directly to Idaho and not wasted time sitting around the hotel in Utah.

Lesson learned. REO Speedwagon and Styx did cancel. We did get a full refund for the concert tickets prior to our trip. We still wanted to get out and see other states, as moving out of California was still in the back of my head. I want to be safe and live in a great community. My neighborhood is changing, and quickly.

Labor Day came and went. I made deals with my resorts for us to perform on multiple days for a lesser rate. I tried to get both Kevin and Anthony booked, but they chose Anthony as a solo act, as he had been their regular performer all these years, and we are very grateful for the opportunity to work the entire weekend.

Another random event happened in September. I do not get mail at my house because I have caught too many people trying to break into my mailbox on security cameras. I get my mail at the PO box. My mailman will not even leave mail if I ask or beg him to. For some odd reason, I received a blank paycheck stub from my mother's work. The moment I saw it I knew what it was, and why it was there. I told Anthony, "It's from my mom." It was from her employer's corporate headquarters in Kentucky, not the local HR down the street. I called them the next day and asked why they would send a blank paycheck stub when my mother had passed five years prior. They said it was a formality. I then also stated the truth: that I had been dealing with the payout of my mother's life insurance since 2015, and it was unresolved. They said they would investigate and get back to me.

CHAPTER 11:
SHOW ME THE MONEY

Anthony and I were pleased to find out we would be transferring to the new ONT1 Amazon on October 4. Our new shift would be Sundays, Mondays, Tuesdays, and Wednesdays from 8:30 p.m. to 12:30 a.m. We were still erring on the side of caution with the optimism that we would be booking shows, and also be working at Amazon on the least probable nights for magic shows. We were excited to have work and rest, and if we felt like picking up extra shifts, there was always VET (voluntary extra time).

At Amazon you get something called UPT (unpaid time off). You start off with thirty hours, and you accrue twenty more every quarter. Somehow Anthony and I had sixty hours saved up. We put in for UPT to go to Utah and Idaho September 13 to 17 knowing we would come back to work and have only one week left of the mandatory six-night-a-week grind before moving on to our new Amazon location.

The transition from LGB5 to ONT1 was seamless. We worked our last shift at LGB5 on Friday, October 2, had Saturday night off, and started at ONT1 on Sunday. It was that easy.

Welcome to ONT1
Photo by Dawn Morgan

In September we also were reaping the rewards of our FREE virtual variety showcases. We (Kevin, Anthony, and I) had booked a school district for every Saturday from September 19 through December 12. We had booked the Colorado communities (plus two other communities in the same development) for virtual performances. We booked the same Roseville senior community where we had had to cancel at the beginning of the year, plus its sister community. I was now the "Ambassador of Kwan," and like Jerry Maguire I was ready to show these boys the money!!

For our first few virtual shows, Anthony and I would set up and tear down each show in my kitchen. This effort took longer than setting up a two-hour Vegas-style illusion show due in part to the backdrop, the sound, the mics, the lights, and the challenge of getting the cameras just right. We decided to gut my formal living room and to set up everything for the show there, leaving the props in their place. We could now just flip a switch and be performance ready. We used the television as our monitor, which made life a lot easier, seeing the audience and its reactions. It is hard not to keep glancing over to watch the show, rather than keeping your eyes, and your eye contact, on the video camera.

For the second time, the whole world was tired of being on lockdown, and Halloween was quickly approaching. Being a magician on Halloween is like being Santa Claus in December. We work!! A lot!! I was starting to field calls, and was out of practice at booking so many shows at once. I made a few mistakes and completely forgot about the weekly virtual school show. I decided to find more entertainers and share the wealth. Plus, Kevin decided he did not want to do school shows any longer. He told us he was returning to cruise ships in mid-November, and then he had his annual contract with Don Laughlin's Riverside Resort and Hotel in Laughlin, Nevada, in December. He decided he would be pulling back from the virtual shows. He did not like them. He missed his live audiences. Another stumbling block for me, but Kevin was going to honor his current bookings, and I would pick up the pieces and move on from there.

We loved working at the new Amazon, and right off the bat we were selected to be learning ambassadors again. Our operations manager also asked us to apply to be production assistants, but that would mean full-time, and at their mercy regarding hours. Anthony wanted to consider it, but the whole point of working at Amazon during the lockdown was to keep the magic going. This was a job for "in the meantime." As flattering as it is for people to think of you as capable, we needed to keep our eye on the ball, as our ball has just started rolling. We were booking shows both virtually and live with social distancing. However, I will say it again: we will be forever grateful to Amazon for its support during this time.

October felt normal. Halloween on Saturday, October 31, sent us into November with renewed enthusiasm.

CHAPTER 12:

HAPPY BIRTHDAY

Novembee 15 is my birthday, and this year I will be
fifty-five. I felt tired. I had not had a manicure, or a
pedicure, or a facial, or a massage. My regular hair salon,
Prim and Proper, was open, and I decided to "GO BIG." I
had been growing out a bob that was looking stringy, so I
made an appointment for hair extensions. When the world
opened the rest of the way, I would look like a magician
assistant, and having big, beautiful hair would take the sting
off fifty-five.

I do not have to tell you we had a big election coming up,
and no matter what side you were on, the stakes were high.

By November 3, Anthony and I had already filled out
our absentee ballots. We drove them to the polling location
near our house, and we handed them over. Now the praying
starts. Please God, let there be peace. Please God, put the
right person in power. Please God, let life return to normal.
Please God, keep us safe.

In 2016 we had voted and gone to the beach. We had a few
drinks and did not listen to the radio or get on our phones.

But hey, it's all about the hair.
Photo by Dawn Morgan

We made this same vow in 2020. We had two virtual shows coming up this week and went home to focus on those.

We had gone from performing twenty shows in October to only eight shows in November. It felt like the world was "on hold." Waiting to see what was going to happen with the election. Waiting to see if COVID would be eradicated. Waiting to see . . .

On the week of my birthday, which fell on a Sunday, we had both Friday and Saturday night shows. Sunday, we worked at Amazon. We decided to hit the beach on Monday, but first we were going to visit with Ken at Magic Galore and

More to see if he had anything "new to us" that we could use for the virtual shows. Not all magic is made for a video camera, and we needed to outthink all the other virtual magicians in what we were presenting. We needed original content.

I did receive a birthday gift from my mom. I went to the PO box and there was a check from Cigna for her life insurance . . . plus interest. I wanted to cry but just could not. I felt that same lost feeling that I did when she passed. I was happy to finally have this money five and a half years later. I knew my mom sent that money when it may be needed the most, even if it was just peace of mind for me to know I had it. I thanked God, I thanked my mom, and I drove straight to the bank and put it in her bank account.

Anthony and I had decided to pick up an extra shift on Thanksgiving. Why not? We had nothing else to do, and it was overtime pay. Holidays and holiday meals have been weird for us without my mom. She always cooked and had the food hot and ready when we were finished performing. That is how my mom and I have operated our entire lives. If my mom, as a single parent, could get work, we would celebrate another day, or we would celebrate when she got off work. Working and getting the bills paid were always our priorities.

Anthony and I had discussed working all night at Amazon and putting the turkey in the oven when we came home so that it could cook while we slept all day. We had discussed buying a Honey Baked ham, but neither of us wanted to wait in a long line to pick it up. We had discussed making our famous steaks from a recipe my childhood friend had given me and that Anthony and I had adopted as our Christmas dinner since 2015. What to do? We ordered two gourmet pizzas and bought our favorite two flavors of ice cream. All in all, we were glad we had ordered the pizzas, because both of our Amazon shifts flexed up. We went to work at 8:30 p.m. on Wednesday and clocked out at 7 a.m. on Thanksgiving. We came home and slept most of the day, waking only to eat our pizza before going back to sleep. Those double shifts on PEAK time really wear you out.

CHAPTER 13:
FALSE POSITIVE?

The pages of the calendar seemed to be turning over quickly. Days were going by fast. We were exhausted most of the time and spent whatever free time we had napping. We did not want to complain to each other, and bring each other down, so we kept looking for ways to change the game and keep our spirits up. Our gym memberships expired. We usually pay cash for both of us at the beginning of the year. I asked the manager of our gym if we could pay in cash for six months now and six months later, as my consumer confidence was not 100 percent and I was technically unemployed. The gym had opened and closed just as much as we had been hired and furloughed. We had not been able to use the spa or locker rooms during COVID. I did not think my request was unreasonable. The gym manager, however, did, and gave us a "No." I decided to work out on my own. I did not need to pay for the gym anyway. After all, I have been out of business now for nine months . . . but really . . . it feels like only fourteen days.

I started off December at 136 pounds. This was up from

129 pounds in December 2019. I ended the year of 2020 at 139 pounds, on New Year's Eve. I had lost all motivation to fit into my magic boxes and my magic costumes. I was not on camera too much for the few virtual shows we had, and I wore yoga pants to work at Amazon. This was the first time in my life I had felt this way, and I was not taking as much pride in myself as I normally do. I had lost all motivation, all optimism, and all hope of life as I knew it ever returning. I was trying to find a solution, but I did not want to grab at straws, and I wasn't sure what the solution could be. Every day I was trying to fight my way out of this paper bag.

We had a few live shows for clients who have booked us every holiday season for sixteen years. So now I am fat, and I have long hair, and I must go perform magic shows outside. To top it off, it was super windy outside. I am grateful for the opportunity to work and perform, but sad to see old friends during this difficult time. It seemed our clients, Anthony, and I were all desperately trying to find comfort in tradition, but nothing about the shows we were performing was traditional. The hardest show was the Newhaven Boys Home. The first Thursday of December is a standing date for them. Every year a group of realtors from San Diego hosts the boys at an entertainment center for food, fun, and celebration. This celebration culminates with the "Anthony the Magic" show and gift exchanges. Since Anthony and I don't really have a family, we consider these clients our family. Every year their show is equivalent to our Thanksgiving or our Christmas with them. This year only one of the realtors was able to come to the boys home to celebrate and see the show. The boys could not be taken off property to the entertainment center, and social gatherings had to be small. I am not sure if the boys ate before or after our show, as Anthony and I were alone outside setting up our show on the blacktop. The boys were great. They were better behaved and happier than most of the young people we perform for. Anthony spent time with them after the show, and we drove home feeling sadder and lonelier than we had before. This was a feeling we would not be able to shake.

Anthony has been a Red Nose Doctor with Healthy Humor at Loma Linda University Children's Hospital for the past year, and he got a lucky break with his Healthy Humor job. They were to have a virtual conference this year, as opposed to the live conference in New York. All the Red Nose Doctors who work at the Loma Linda children's hospital would be paid to attend the online conference for three days and learn new ways to entertain in the virtual world. How great is that. Getting paid and learning from others how to entertain online. Sold!

It is during the time of Anthony's conference that I decided to keep myself busy by promoting the virtual shows. I also made it my personal mission to get booked virtually at the world-famous Hollywood Magic Castle. Anthony and I had been watching its Saturday night shows, and we felt we could do just as good a job as the magicians we were watching, so, "Why not us?" I started my email campaign. I am not going to lie: our Magic Castle dues of $410 was also due during this time. In my mind, I was not going to renew if we were not considered for a spot in the show. We often feel like outsiders at the Magic Castle, and it seems more difficult for us than most to book a performance there. We have felt this way for a few years, and every year when that renewal comes, we ask ourselves, "Is this money well spent?"

Magic Castle entertainment director Jack Goldfinger wanted to see a current virtual show video. I sent a video of Kevin and Anthony performing a fantastic holiday show. Jack wanted an unedited cut of the exact fifteen minutes we would present for the Magic Castle. I could not find the four effects back-to-back in any of the shows I had recorded, so I sent four effects that were back-to-back and asked for Anthony's forgiveness later. Like I said, we had really worked on our content and knew we were not replicating what other magicians were performing virtually.

Jack called us and said he loved the video, and could we perform on January 23, 2021? Relieved to get a spot so quickly, we said yes. Jack asked if we knew of two acts we worked well with who could perform with us. We told him of course: Kevin Johnson and Robert Baxt. Both Kevin and Robert had been performing with us in the *Ultimate Virtual Variety Show* I was booking, and we all knew each other's tendencies, material, and timing. This would be a great show. He told us to have them send a video ASAP and he would

The Magic Castle . . . virtually
Photo by Dawn Morgan

work it out.

I was very happy that we were building the Ultimate Virtual Variety Show. I felt proud when I could book other entertainers. I felt like a boss. I called Kevin and Robert, and they happily went to work on their videos for Jack.

I do not know what happened, but Jack felt Robert was not ready yet, and called us to ask if we knew of anyone else while Robert tweaked his show. I felt bad, but Robert did not have the advantage of working with Paul Beach from Legoland. Anthony and I gave him as many tips as we had implemented into our virtual show, and we knew he would get booked eventually. We did know of another magician, who lived down the street, Martin Lewis. Martin could come to our house and be in our Zoom studio with us. Thus, lighting and sound wouldn't be a problem. We called Martin, and he agreed to come on board. Jack approved of this trio immediately, and we were confirmed. Jack had a lot of great ideas, including using Kevin's drawing board and Martin's card rise with callbacks to each other. We knew this was going to be a great show. I paid our Magic Castle dues and started to promote this show with everything I had.

The rest of December sort of muddled along. We were working extra hours and extra hard at Amazon, as it was "peak" time due to Christmas. We had a lot of shows booked that we were working around, and we were learning a lot of new technology. Now we were finding clients who not only wanted shows on Zoom, but also on Google Suites and Microsoft Teams. Pivot, Pivot, Pivot.

The last ten days of December we did not perform magic shows at all. At first, the shows we had booked canceled due to COVID on their end. It also seems that when the world thinks we are about to open, requests for shows decrease. I take that as people thinking, "I will not book this virtual show because I may be able to have it live if I wait another month." Then something extremely unfortunate happened. The Wednesday before Christmas Eve, Anthony and I were working in small sort at Amazon. We finished our work in time, and were asked to teach a class of ten. I did not want to, so went to stage pallets. Anthony took one for the team and taught the class. The following Saturday, Anthony felt very tired and very sore. I fed him all the best food I could think of. I bought vitamins, aspirin, green smoothie drinks, and lemon water. I kept taking his temperature. It was nothing big, 99.5. At work it must be 100.4 to be sent home. He could smell and he could taste, so I just figured he was sore and tired from working so hard at Amazon. Heck, we had spent the last nine months being sore and tired. How would we know the difference?

Anthony stayed home from work for the next two days, and I went in. I felt fine. We decided we would both go and get tested. My test came back immediately that day. Negative. Anthony's test did not come back for two days. Positive. We emailed Amazon. They said I could come to work, but Anthony could not for fourteen days. We called what few shows we had on the books and alerted them to the situation. We both tested again five days later, and we both tested negative. Happy New Year!

CHAPTER 14:
A Very Merry Unchristmas

A ♥

A ♣

A ♠

A ♦

In December I had started applying for jobs in marketing and promotions with a few local casinos. January got off to a slow start. I was restless at Amazon. I had realized "fourteen days" was about to turn into a full-blown year. I did not mind working at Amazon for fifteen dollars an hour in the meantime, but now this was a year out of my life. I applied at three different casinos in the promotions and marketing department. I needed a job that could use my talents, my experience, and my education, with a company that could pay me what I was worth. I was feeling anxious and just wanted to do whatever I could to move life forward.

Anthony must have felt the same way, because without mentioning it to me, he found the busiest place in town to get a job. The morgue. Our friend and mentor John Pooley had passed, and we were to attend his service on Monday, January 18. Anthony called the mortuary to confirm times for the service and asked if they were hiring. They were not, but transportation was. Anthony was hired on the spot for a trial run. He would start that Saturday night, as we did not

With Mr. and Mrs. Pooley at Welk Theatre
Photo courtesy of John Pooley

have one magic show on the books.

Joe Biden was going to be the country's new president. Everyone was just waiting to see what was going to happen next.

I spent 100 percent of my time promoting the Magic Castle show. Each performer was allotted six complimentary tickets to invite guests to the show. We all agreed to save those spots for potential entertainment bookers to come to the virtual show and see what we could do for their clients in front of a real audience.

I also put us on a site called Groupon. This is a major entertainment discount site. I figured . . . why not? It was better than nothing. I did whatever I could to change my chi and bring good energy.

Then the worst thing happened. The night before the Magic Castle show, while we were rehearsing online with

Magic Castle, someone from Facebook went on a private page and disparaged our show. We did not need that stress. Getting a Magic Castle booking does not come easily for us, and we did not need any negativity from someone we did not even know. At the end of our Magic Castle rehearsal, I picked up my phone and had a message from Michael Mezmer alerting me to the situation. Anthony called up the person who posted the disparaging remark and had an honest discussion with her. She removed the post, and we were somewhat relieved. I am not going to lie; we held our breath the entire next day in case Jack called and pulled us from the show over this negative comment.

Saturday, January 23, came, and we slept in, we put on face masks, we drank water, we prayed, and we prepared our show three times to make sure we did not miss a beat. We meditated and visualized. We just wanted to get this day over with. Once the show started, it seemed to go by in a flash, but Anthony was perfect. He gave a standing-ovation, emotionally charged performance. Anthony performed Lemon/Canary, Bill in Sugar, Cue the Magic!, and his Snowing Tribute. During the snowing tribute, Anthony gave respect to all the great magicians we lost in 2020, but most importantly to Mr. John Pooley. After the show was over and we were packing up with Martin in our living room, Jack called. Jack was very happy and said over the phone, " . . . and now you can consider this your dress rehearsal and take the next one serious." Jack told us to put together another performance with different content and send it his way. This show, for us, was satisfying like no other.

The end of January carried on with the good vibes. We performed at a local Christian school for PTA family night and did a great job. We performed for a new community in Colorado and did a great job. Then we received an email from Gay Blackstone asking us to submit material for *Masters of Illusion*! We were back in the saddle again.

CHAPTER 15:
BOOTSTRAPPING?

Over the weekend I received a last-minute call for Tuesday, February 2. This was a client we had performed for in the past, and we thought it would be fun to include Kevin in the show and split the pay with him. We love performing with Kevin, and this client owns his own theater in Carlsbad, so it would be great if we could bring "Comedy & Magic" to Carlsbad when the world opens again. If not, then virtually we could do "Comedy & Magic, Live from Carlsbad."

The next day the client called me and asked if we knew of another performer who could do a show on the following evening, February 3, for the same group. Even better. Anthony and I performed the show on the second, and we gave the show on the third to Kevin. We both had the opportunity to work and make full pay, and the client would be able to see Kevin's show in its entirety.

One of the casinos I had applied to called me for an interview, so things were looking up. Amazon was slow after the holidays. Every shift they were offering VTO (voluntary time off). Anthony had his job with transportation at the morgue, and he seemed to like it. They worked from 9 p.m. until the wee hours of the morning. I think what he liked most was his boss, Roger, and the conversations they would have on those long drives in the middle of the night. The job I am not so sure about. Now only if I too could have a job that paid more and still made time for the magic shows that came in.

The Groupon specials were booking, and we now were performing for places that would have never heard of us if not for Groupon. We performed for families in Ohio, Arizona, New Jersey, and South Africa! Groupon took most of the money, but we were performing for people to whom we could not otherwise promote ourselves, and it was more than we would make anywhere else. One show we performed had guests in three different time zones: 9:00 a.m. in California

My formal living room, now our virtual studio
Photo by Dawn Morgan

and Arizona, noon in New Jersey, and 6:00 p.m. in South Africa!! Where else but on Zoom could you perform in three different time zones simultaneously?

Anthony and I had decided maybe we needed a small road trip, and Sedona, Arizona, would be a place we could drive to and spend just a few days. We wanted to hike, to be with nature, and to get our chakras balanced.

We had emailed Jack regarding another Magic Castle booking, with no word back. We even made a second video, with different content, and sent it over. We had also sent content to Gay Blackstone for *Masters of Illusion*. Also no word back. We checked in with both of them via email to ensure they had received our correspondence and content, but our inquiries went unanswered. Thank goodness we were so happy with our last Magic Castle performance. There was no doubt in our minds that our show was good. I am sure there are tons of magicians trying to get a spot, and Jack is very busy and wants to give everyone a turn. Normally, Anthony and I would sit and stew over what we had done so wrong that we were undeserving of a response. We are working hard on learning to let it go.

Valentine's Day came and went like any other day. We performed a virtual show, had lunch, took a nap, and went to Amazon. We had bought a Groupon for ourselves to go dolphin and whale watching, and we would be doing that in the following week. The day after Valentine's Day I received a text from the general manager of Castle Park. "Can you call me?" I do not know why, but texts like that always stress me out.

I called Ken back, and he told me Castle Park was not able to hire me back yet for group sales and marketing, but Palace Entertainment had two FECs (family entertainment centers) that could use my help part-time. They could pay me my former hourly wage, and I could market for Boomers Vista and Boomers Palm Springs. We would have to figure out the logistics if I accepted the offer. I wondered if the casino had called to check my references with Ken, but no matter, I wanted to go back to what I did well. Absolutely, yes!

Anthony and I were in a very celebratory mood. We went out twice that week. Once to watch the dolphins and then later that week we went to a place where there was live music, and we drank and danced all night. Anthony spent a ton of money on food and drinks, but we did not care. We were taking our lives back.

CHAPTER 16:
ONE FULL YEAR!

March 1: I started working back at my old desk at Castle Park. We decided the best way for me to work for the two Boomers locations was to work locally at Castle Park. Each Boomers location was an hour drive from my house, and each was in the opposite direction from the other. I work Mondays, Wednesdays, and Fridays, and my schedule is flexible in case I book a magic show for Anthony. I am very lucky, and Castle Park has been very good to Anthony and me.

Anthony and I have mostly given up on watching television or the news, or scrolling Facebook when we are bored. My friend Connie had asked me to be a guest speaker at her social media summit, Social Summit 2021, and I agreed. Anthony and I had been spending our time listening to all the guest speakers at Connie's summit during our drives and at home. We had new hope and optimism for our future online. Connie had asked me for something to put in the "digital goodie bag," and I had nothing to offer except for a free Zoom magic show . . . and this book I have been writing. I have twenty-seven half-started books from over the years, but have not finished one. Just finishing this book seemed like a daunting task.

After Connie's summit, Anthony and I started listening to multiple podcasts, lectures, and inspirational talks wherever we could find them. Everyone had something interesting to say. We were trying to bring in only positivity.

We would walk at the park almost every day. One lap would equal twenty-five hundred steps. We were trying for four laps a day; not that four laps were too many, but we get anxious with our time and always want to be accomplishing something. Usually, two laps are the max before we want to get home and get working.

On Friday, March 5, I was working at my desk at Castle Park when I went to ask Laura in human resources a question. She asked if I had heard the news. (I had heard news, but was not sure which news she was talking about.) Laura said Disneyland and other outdoor venues will be allowed to open on April 1. This is April Fool's Day, so I hope this is no joke. This is, however, very good news.

While the news was good, it made Anthony and me a bit anxious. We were to go to Sedona March 18 to 21. It was a small trip, but now we wanted to be home, and be ready, in case our phones started ringing again.

We had listened to two lecturers we really liked. We decided to take the Sedona money and invest in coaching from the two speakers and what they had to say. Now we realized our website, which we had loved for the past six years, needed a makeover. Connie had built that website for us in 2015, and it had done so much for us that pre-COVID we did not have to look for work. We had six hundred shows a year on rotation, and that was due in part to whatever magic spell

Connie had waved over our website. Now we needed to adjust the website to include the virtual shows.

I cannot believe we are one week away from March 13 and one year of lockdown. I cannot believe how fast this year went. I cannot believe that this may all well be over. I cannot believe this all happened in the first place.

CHAPTER 17:

CAUTIOUSLY OPTIMISTIC

Kevin told us during one of our Saturday performances in February that he had been rehired at Legoland for twenty dates in March. While we are a little bit jealous, he does have a family of five children to feed, and we do have our own regular venues that should soon be calling for our shows.

I called Arty Loon and Robert Baxt to ask if they could fill in for Kevin at the virtual shows I had booked for him.

March was another slow month for shows. We performed a few Boy Scout Blue and Gold events and our regular weekly school shows, but other than that . . . nada.

The March 13 anniversary date came and went without much fanfare. Anthony and I tried to keep our nose to the grindstone and to keep working on updating our website. We are not techies. We were scared to death to ruin Connie's work. We watched so many tutorials, sat in on so many lectures, and bickered with each other just a little.

We tried to enjoy this downtime, because we know how life is when we are working. We go, go, go all day every day performing shows and running the errands that go along with owning our own business. We have learned to set aside time and have enjoyed several small vacations over the years. Although this past year would be considered time off from work by many, for us it has not been. We have worked the entire year, scrambling to keep our business alive.

We had been using the "wings," or side curtains, from Castle Park as our backdrop in our studio. Now we needed to clean them again and return them to the park. We ordered our own curtains, this time in blue velvet, as we have virtual shows booked through 2021. The black curtains we use at our regular shows just do not show up well on television.

We bit the bullet and joined the gym because my weight had now gone up to 144 pounds. I don't even know how this happened, and Anthony is just as baffled. It felt good to be able to do unlimited cardio once again. I have been athletic my entire life. To not be able to go ice skating, to the gym, to dance class, or to boot camp has been rough on me and my mood.

I am enjoying working at Boomers! Vista and Boomers! Palm Springs. I love the people at both parks, and this is the one thing that excites me and makes me feel positive. I am already booking small groups to come to the park, so I can see I do make a difference.

While we were driving home from Boomers Vista on March 26, Castle Park's general manager called to ask if I could send out a press release. Castle Park is going to reopen on April 9. I do not want to assume that means we will be performing magic shows again that soon, but it is a good sign. We will be doing a test run at the park for "friends and family" on Wednesday, April 7. I hurried home to call all my friends in the media and get the information out.

As of today, March 27, I am down to 138 pounds. I had a manager meeting on Microsoft Teams with my director at Palace Entertainment, and she showed me the banners Castle Park had ordered for the parking lot. "25 Years of Magic" at Castle Park, and they used Anthony's photo. We had not been forgotten. It is time to celebrate. It is time to get back to work.

Promoting the April 9 reopening of Castle Park on ABC news
Photo by Dawn Morgan

BOOK ANTHONY THE MAGIC

AT ANTHONYTHEMAGIC.COM

ACKNOWLEDGMENTS

Thank you to *Anthony Hernandez* for giving me a job, a life, and always something new on my to-do list.

Thank you to *Connie Woods* for showing up for me, encouraging me, pushing me, and making the introduction to Scott Ryan.

To *Scott Ryan*, my designer, and *David Bushman*, my editor, your patience in this process was greatly appreciated.

To *Michael Mezmer* for writing the foreword with very short notice, and to *Kelsi Barnett* for taking time out of a three-day trip to California for an unexpected photo shoot.

Thank you to everyone who believed in me, gave me an opportunity, and looked the other way when I took on too much.

I want to thank all my close friends, fans, and audience members who came to see us over the years, and sat in on our practice shows during COVID.

We want to thank our venues that kept in contact with us over the past year and half despite their own challenges, including Castle Park, Tom's Farms, Welk Resort Theatre, Marriott Newport Coast Villas, Marriott Shadow Ridge, Marriott Desert Spring Villas, Hyatt Huntington Beach, Monarch Resort Laguna, Live Oak Canyon Pumpkin Patch, and the World Famous Hollywood Magic Castle. You are like family to us, and we have enjoyed the many years we have worked with you.

To every entertainment booker whom I harassed via email to invite to the Ultimate Virtual Variety Showcase.

To our friends and peers in the entertainment industry who were scrambling just as hard as we were to keep the dream alive when we didn't know what the next step would be, or if life would ever return to normal.

I would love to name each and every person individually, but there just aren't enough pages for all the blessings in my life. Thank You.

ABOUT THE AUTHOR

Born and raised in Southern California by a single, self-supporting mother, Dawn Morgan has mastered the art of being self-sufficient and creating something out of nothing. Always in the right place at the right time, Dawn landed her first job at the age of twelve, cleaning beauty shops after school, earning enough money to take ice skating lessons and compete locally. Dawn graduated from California Baptist University, Riverside, in 1994 with a Bachelor of Science degree and later earned her teaching credential while performing with the NHL's newly minted hockey franchise, the Mighty Ducks.

Dawn worked in professional sports and media for several years before arriving at Castle Amusement Park in 2004 where she met Anthony Hernandez. The two have become one of the most-sought-after magic and illusion acts in California, appearing in over six hundred shows a year for the past seventeen years.

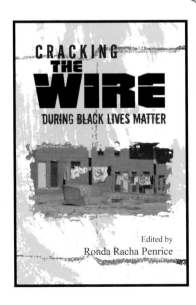